The Financially Healthy Mind

Mind

Overcoming Money Stress

Table of Contents

Chapter 1. Introduction

Welcome to "The Financially Healthy Mind: Overcoming Money Stress," an enlightening Special Report designed to enhance your monetary well-being! This vibrant resource isn't just about numbers and equations, it is your roadmap to financial tranquility. It artfully weaves the often complicated realm of financial management with the simple, everyday principles of mental wellness. This synergy helps to overcome stressors and build a future of financial security with an energized spirit. Feel inspired as you gain clarity on financial complexities, implement effective money management strategies, and uncover secrets to maintaining a financially healthy mindset. This isn't about instant riches; it's about serenity, resilience, and empowerment in your financial journey. Get ready to turn the page to a more confident, financially savvy you! So why wait? This Special Report stands as an investment in yourself and your brilliantly prosperous future.

Chapter 2. Shaping Your Financially Healthy Mindset

We all have a unique relationship with money, built over a lifetime of experiences and influences. To shape a mindset that complements and supports financial well-being, it is essential to understand these influences and learn how to manage and channel them into productive viewpoints. This involves understanding your financial beliefs, needs, aspirations, and fears.

2.1. Understanding Your Relationship with Money

Each of us interacts with money in different ways. Some may see it as a means to an end, while for others, it may represent security, power, or freedom. Your perspectives about money are largely shaped by how you were raised, what you were taught about money, and your life experiences.

Understanding these influences is the first step towards shaping a financially healthy mindset. Reflect on your past and present behaviors around money. Do you tend to spend as soon as you receive it, or do you hoard cash out of fear for the future? Your behavior patterns can provide you with valuable insights and serve as a starting point to shape a healthier relationship with your finances.

Begin by listing your perceptions and beliefs about money. Identify patterns that steer your financial decisions. By clearly defining these patterns, you can start working on breaking any detrimental habits and promoting healthy ones.

2.2. Setting Your Financial Goals

Knowing what you are aiming for in your financial life is immensely beneficial for your monetary mindset. These could be short-term goals like saving for a vacation or longer-term ones like retirement planning. Having a clear vision of your financial future helps you stay focused and motivated.

When setting your financial goals, be specific. Instead of "I want to save money," a more effective goal would be "I want to save $5000 for a down payment on a car by next year."

Remember to set goals that are realistic and attainable within your timeframe. Using the SMART (Specific, Measurable, Achievable, Relevant, and Time-bound) technique can help you here. Regularly review your goals to ensure they align with your changing needs and circumstances.

2.3. Crafting Your Financial Plan

Once your goals are set, you can work on a comprehensive plan to achieve them. A solid financial plan includes budgeting, saving strategies, investment opportunities, and provision for unforeseen circumstances.

A budget is a fundamental tool in your financial plan. It provides a clear overview of your income versus your expenses, helping you monitor your spending and identifying areas where you can make savings.

While crafting your financial plan, educate yourself on the different investment opportunities that align with your goals. Diversifying your portfolio can provide you with different revenue streams and cushion you against a sudden financial shock. If you're unsure about investing, speak to a financial adviser for professional guidance.

2.4. Cultivating an Attitude of Gratitude

A critical aspect of a financially healthy mindset is expressing gratitude for what you already have. It may seem counterintuitive, but considering how fortunate you are in certain aspects of your life can mitigate feelings of scarcity, limit reckless spending, and inspire you to invest wisely.

Studies have found that cultivating an attitude of gratitude can increase financial patience and reduce impulsive spending. The more you learn to appreciate what you have, the less you seek to find happiness in spending on unnecessary items. This distinct shift to conscious consumption bolsters your budget and savings, moving you one step closer to your financial goals.

2.5. Building Resilience

Financial resilience is about building buffers and safety nets. Whether it's an emergency fund for unexpected costs, diversifying investment to mitigate risks, or ensuring you're adequately insured, financial resilience provides a sense of control over your financial future.

Building financial resilience is not a one-day task; it involves repeated habits and consistent effort. The habit of saving, the discipline of sticking to budgets, the prudence in making financial decisions all add up.

2.6. Developing a Growth Mindset

A financially healthy mindset also involves embracing a growth mindset, challenging the fixed mindset which views ability and success as inherent or set in stone. With a growth mindset, one holds a belief that intelligence can develop with time and effort; therefore, financial skills are not static, and one continually acquires new strategies for wealth management.

By taking the time to understand, learn, and continually grow, you will find that financial planning becomes less intimidating, transformed into an empowering and enriching journey.

2.7. Promoting Mindfulness

Mindfulness is the art of being fully present and engaged in the current moment. In terms of maintaining a financially healthy mindset, this practice translates into making conscious financial decisions.

Rather than making hasty purchases or immediately succumbing to sales or discounts, mindfulness encourages you to pause and consider the consequences of these decisions. As a result, you develop a wiser, more intentional relationship with money.

In conclusion, shaping a financially healthy mindset requires understanding your past and present relationship with money, setting and working towards financial goals, learning and building financial resilience, and cultivating attitudes of gratitude, mindfulness, and growth. By consistently applying these principles, you can enhance your monetary wellness, overcome financial stressors, and establish a future of financial security.

Chapter 3. Understanding the Connection Between Money and Stress

The ancient philosopher Seneca once commented, "It is not the man who has too little, but the man who craves more, that is poor." Money is a necessity in modern society, facilitating most of our day-to-day transactions. However, when money becomes a source of stress, it affects every aspect of our lives including our relationships, performance at work, and mental health.

3.1. The Psychology of Money

The relationship between our mind and money is complex and influenced by a variety of factors. It is intertwined with our emotions, beliefs, and attitudes that we've developed over time. Many of these thoughts are implicit, formed unconsciously based on our observations and experiences as we navigate through life.

Remember that money is a tool, a means to an end, not an end in itself. It should serve us, not the other way around. Therefore, it's critical to develop a healthy relationship with money. To achieve this, it's important to understand the psychological aspects of money; dispelling money myths, recognizing your money scripts, and ultimately reshaping your financial behaviors.

3.2. The Impact of Money Stress on Health

Unexpected expenses, debt, lack of savings, or retirement crisis - whatever your source of financial worry might be it is important to understand that excessive concern over finances can take a toll on our well-being. Chronic financial stress can lead to severe health issues such as insomnia, depression, anxiety, high blood pressure, heart diseases, and much more. Research also shows that financial stress can affect our cognitive abilities, causing difficulty in making sound financial decisions, thus creating a vicious cycle of money troubles and mental distress.

Taggart, an economic psychologist, says people handle money stress in different ways; for some, it's a challenge, for others, it's a threat. The trick is to transform your monetary stress into economic eustress (healthy stress) by taking active steps in managing your finances and gaining financial literacy.

3.3. Understanding Your Money Scripts

A significant element in the correlation between finances and stress is the concept of 'Money Scripts,' a term coined by psychologist Dr. Brad Klontz. Money Scripts refer to the unconscious beliefs about money that we inherit from our family, culture, and experiences. These could span from 'money is the root of all evil' to 'money brings happiness.'

Awareness of your money scripts can help you identify the root cause of your financial behavior. For example, if you have an avoidance money script, you are more likely to ignore financial decisions, leading to financial problems and subsequent stress. By understanding your money scripts, you can reshape your monetary habits by challenging these subconscious financial biases.

3.4. Strategies for Overcoming Money Stress

Now that we've explored the psychological factors influencing money stress, let's dive into strategies to overcome it.

1. **Budgeting:** One of the most effective methods to overcome financial stress is through budgeting. It provides you with an overview of your income, expenses, and savings.

2. **Emergency Savings:** An often overlooked yet likely a key stressor is the lack of an emergency fund. Setting aside a portion of your income for unexpected expenses can give you peace of mind.

3. **Debt Management:** If you're in debt, work out a manageable repayment plan. Consider talking to a debt advisor to structure an effective debt repayment plan that fits your budget.

4. **Financial Planning:** Having clear financial goals and developing a roadmap to reach them can significantly decrease your stress levels.

5. **Professional Guidance:** Don't hesitate to seek help from financial professionals. They can assist you in managing complicated financial aspects like investments, taxes, and retirement planning.

Remember, overcoming money stress doesn't happen overnight but by taking proactive steps and making informed financial decisions, you can ensure a healthy money mindset and a stress-free life.

Finally, it's crucial to outline that one size doesn't fit all. What works for one may not work for others. Therefore, understanding your personal financial situation and aligning it with your lifestyle is of paramount importance.

In the end, money is an essential element of our lives. It provides us with the means to live comfortably and supports our goals and dreams. However, it should not become a source of chronic stress. Understanding your relationship with money and harnessing strategies to manage financial stress is a critical step towards achieving your financial harmony and wellness. Treat money as a tool you control, rather than a power that controls you, and rest will fall into place on its journey.

In conclusion, while the connection between money and stress can be strong, a deeper understanding and implementation of strategic changes can work powerful transformations. It's not about accumulating wealth; it's about achieving a financially healthy and stress-free life. You have the power to conquer your financial worries and emerge as a more confident, financially savvy individual ready to face any monetary challenge that comes your way. This is your journey to financial tranquility.

Chapter 4. Destigmatizing Money Conversations: Openness Leads to Growth

A prevailing issue within our society is the discomfort or downright taboo that surrounds money conversations. In households, schools, and even workplaces, discussing finances, salary, and personal wealth can often feel uncomfortable. It's as though an invisible barrier prohibits open exchanges on financial matters. The first step in destigmatizing money conversations is understanding why this has become a societal norm and identifying methods to counteract these barriers.

4.1. Understanding the Money Taboo

The taboo around money discussions is deeply rooted in societal norms and individual beliefs. Many people associate money conversations with bragging, showing off, or revealing too much about their personal life. For others, it can involve feelings of inadequacy or fears of being judged.

Historically, money has been a topic confined to hushed-toned discussions and hidden from everyday conversation due to perceived notions of politeness. In many family environments, parents often hesitate to discuss finances with their kids, either to protect them from worry or because they themselves feel uncomfortable with the topic. These silences can often be harmful and foster a culture of financial ignorance, leaving individuals ill-prepared to handle their financial well-being.

4.2. Overcoming the Fear of Judgment

Often, the hesitance to discuss finances is driven by the fear of judgment. Whether it's a fear of appearing unsuccessful, not financially savvy, or incapable of managing money, these fears inhibit open conversations about money. The reality, though, is that everyone is on their own financial journey, with unique goals, challenges, and perspectives. It is important to remember that everyone starts somewhere, and ongoing learning and growth is a part of this journey.

The key to overcoming the fear of judgment and destigmatizing money conversations is cultivating an environment of understanding and empathy. If a conversation feels safe, supportive, and free of judgment, it can empower individuals to openly discuss their financial concerns, triumphs, plans, and doubts.

In practical terms: cultivate money conversations with friends and family, discuss personal financial successes and pitfalls, share learning resources about financial management, and invite others to do the same.

4.3. Financial Education and Openness

When it comes to financial education, the saying "knowledge is power" truly applies. Greater understanding of personal finances, financial markets, and economic trends can increase confidence and destigmatize money conversations.

By committing ourselves to continuous education about money matters, we can not only normalize these conversations but also make better financial decisions. There are many resources available, including books, courses, webinars, podcasts, and personal finance blogs. Having a strong financial education acts as a catalyst to promote open dialogues about money, reducing associated stress and anxiety.

4.4. Fostering a Culture of Financial Transparency

Building a culture of financial transparency is pivotal to eradicating the stigma around money discussions. Transparency promotes openness, inclusivity, and empowerment. A transparent culture can be developed within family units, social groups, or even workplaces.

At home, parents can involve their children in money conversations at an early age, fostering a home environment where children grow up understanding money management. A family's approach to financial transparency can help children become more financially literate adults.

On a societal level, workplaces could lead by example in fostering a culture of salary transparency which can help mitigate wage gaps and provide employees a more realistic understanding of their worth in the job market.

4.5. Destigmatizing Money Conversations: The Journey to Growth

In conclusion, destigmatizing money conversations is much more than being able to speak freely about our financial lives. It is an empowering journey of education, openness, and growth. The journey should be seen as a continuous process that involves educating oneself and others, supporting transparency, and fostering an environment where money discussions are seen as normal, worthwhile, and empowering.

On this journey, we not only learn and grow as individuals but also help others along the way by sharing our knowledge and insights, breaking the cycle of financial ignorance. This journey allows us to shape not just our own financial futures, but also forge a new societal norm where openness about money leads to financial wellness.

By breaking the money taboo, we can initiate conversations that shape our financial health and futures in a positive and productive manner. And remember, every conversation, no matter how small it may seem, contributes to the overall mission of destigmatizing money discussions. When we, as a society, can openly discuss our relationship with money and break the chains of financial secrecy, we empower ourselves and others to create a future of financial independence, resilience, and security.

Chapter 5. Embracing Financial Independence: Empowering Steps Toward Money Autonomy

"Embracing financial independence" denotes walking a path where earning, saving, investing, and spending are conscious and empowered decisions. It's a life where you aren't bogged down by financial stresses but uplifted by your capability to navigate through life's fiscal twists and turns. It is, quite simply, an area where you call the shots—ensuring not just your survival, but your prosperity.

5.1. Understanding Financial Independence

The term "financial independence" may evoke images of millionaires lounging on yachts. However, financial independence has a more pragmatic and attainable ideal: it's about having enough financial resources to make choices that allow you to enjoy life and prepare for any uncertainties without undue stress.

Working towards financial independence means creating a financial cushion that can withstand unexpected expenses or income losses, covering day-to-day costs with ease, and having the freedom to make lifestyle choices as per your preferences.

5.2. Taking Stock of Your Financial Situation

A crucial first step towards financial independence is understanding your current financial position. A comprehensive review of your finances includes a clear snapshot of your income, expenses, assets, and liabilities. This provides a foundation on which to build and grow.

1. Income: This includes consistent resources like salaries, business income, and part-time job earnings. Irregular sources such as dividends, capital gains, or bonuses are also a part of your income.

2. Expenses: These are your monthly outflows, including rent/mortgage, utilities, food, transportation, health care, debt payments, entertainment, and any other spending categories.

3. Assets: These are all your ownings that have value - home, car, savings, investments, and any other properties.

4. Liabilities: These are your debts and obligations, like student loans, car loans, credit card debt, and mortgage.

Once this picture is clear, you can set relevant and achievable goals, guiding your journey towards financial independence.

5.3. Crafting a Comprehensive Budget

Once you have a clear understanding of your financial situation, craft a budget. This should categorize your income and outlays, helping optimize saving and spending. A good budget is both flexible and strict—allowing ease of adjustment in changing situations but keeping non-negotiable expenses and savings as fixed as possible.

1. Income: Total all income sources to understand your complete earnings.

2. Expenses: Categorize your expenses into non-discretionary (like housing, utilities, essential groceries, and medications) and

discretionary spending (like eating out, vacations, and shopping).

3. Savings: Always factor savings into your budget. A thumb rule is to save at least 20% of your income every month.

4. Investments: Consider investing a portion of your money for potential higher returns.

A comprehensive budget reminds you to live within your means. Consistently sticking to this budget is key to reaching financial independence.

5.4. Building an Emergency Fund

An emergency fund—cash set aside to cover unexpected expenses or financial emergencies—is a crucial pillar of financial independence. It provides a safety net in case of job loss, medical emergencies, urgent major expenses, or unexpected drops in income.

Ideally, your emergency fund should cover 3-6 months' worth of living expenses. You might start small, even setting aside a few dollars every week can add up over time. Having this security ensures financial independence isn't compromised during unforeseen circumstances.

5.5. Paying Off Debts

Debt is the greatest impediment to financial independence. The longer it lasts, the more you end up paying—compromising your saving and investing capacity.

Define a debt-payment strategy:

1. The Avalanche Method attacks high-interest debt first, gradually moving to the lower ones.

2. The Snowball Method suggests paying off small debts first,

gaining momentum as each one is paid off.

3. The Stack Method is a mixture of both, focusing on paying off small high-interest debts first.

Choose the strategy that works best for your situation. Remember, prompt and consistent debt-payment helps engrain financial discipline crucial for financial independence.

5.6. Investments and Wealth Growth

Proliferating wealth pushes you further along the road to financial independence. Effective wealth growth involves putting your money to work through investments. These could include stocks, bonds, mutual funds, real estate, or starting your own business.

Investing might seem intimidating at first, with risks involved. However, a balanced, diversified portfolio can help mitigate these risks. Always do your research, consult with financial advisors, or use robo-advisors if starting out.

5.7. Review and Adjust

Finally, regularly reviewing your financial plan and adjusting your strategies help anchor your journey to financial independence. Quarterly or half-yearly reviews can aid in finding gaps, analysing wins and losses, and making necessary course corrections.

Embracing financial independence means consciously engaging finances and making empowered decisions that cater to your present and future goals. Each step you take on this journey paves the way for a financially self-reliant and worry-free life.

Chapter 6. Strategic Budgeting: Making Money Work for You

Budgeting plays an integral role in a healthy financial life. It is the process where you recognize what you're spending your money on, and how much of it you're using up. But, when executed strategically, budgeting becomes a powerful tool that makes your money work for you. It effectively sets the stage, enabling you to achieve monetary tranquility and resilience.

6.1. The Concept of Strategic Budgeting

Strategic budgeting is not just about counting money or cutting costs. It is a comprehensive approach where you align your financial activities with your goals. Similar to how businesses use strategic planning to achieve their objectives, you employ this method to enhance your personal finances.

There are five key steps in strategic budgeting: Setting Goals, Gathering Data, Analyzing and Planning, Implementing, and Monitoring. By following these steps, you will transform your budget into a dynamic tool that propels you towards your financial goals.

1. **Setting Goals**: Your financial journey should always start with a goal. What are you aiming for? It could be anything from saving for retirement, buying a new car, to paying off student loans. Write down your short, medium, and long-term financial goals; then prioritize them based on your current situation and future aspirations.

2. **Gathering Data**: Collect and review your financial data. This

includes your income, expenses, assets, and liabilities. By doing so, you have a clear picture of your current financial status, which is an essential first step in creating a realistic budget.

3. **Analyzing and Planning**: In this step, you'll determine how to allocate your resources to meet your goals. You'll need to assess your expenses and identify areas where you might cut back. Also, you should consider how to maximize your income. This might mean finding a side job, investing, or perhaps starting a small business.

4. **Implementing**: Once you have a plan, it's time to put it into action. This requires discipline and consistency. Be sure to stick to your budget, make necessary adjustments, and reprioritize expenses when needed.

5. **Monitoring**: Track your progress regularly. It not only helps you stay on course, but it also provides you an opportunity to revise your budget in light of changes in your financial situation or goals.

6.2. Implementing a Zero-Based Budget

Strategic budgeting can be implemented in many ways. One popular and effective method is the zero-based budget.

The principal concept here drives home the idea that every single dollar has a purpose. At the end of the month, your income minus your outgoings should equate to zero. This doesn't mean you're spending all that you earn, but instead you're allocating every dollar to a specific category, whether it's for expenses, saving, investing, or debt repayment.

Here is how a zero-based budget might look:

1. Personal Income+: $4000

2. Rent or Mortgage: -$1200

3. Groceries: -$400

4. Utilities: -$300

5. Transportation: -$500

6. Entertainment: -$200

7. Emergency Fund: -$500

8. Investment for Retirement: -$500

9. Student Loan: -$400

10. Remaining Balance: $0

This kind of budgeting promotes financial discipline and ensures that you're steering every dollar to where it brings added value.

6.3. Using Technology to Your Advantage

In the digital age, make use of technology to streamline your budgeting process.

There are numerous budgeting apps and tools available that can connect to your bank accounts, categorize your spending automatically, set up and track your budgets, and even send you alerts when you're nearing your limits.

Such tools offer a considerable advantage, as they provide clear visibility of your finances at your fingertips, enable informed decision-making, and, importantly, save you time. A few of the popular options include YNAB (You Need a Budget), Mint, and PocketGuard.

Remember, though, while these tools can provide valuable support, the key to successful budgeting still lies in your discipline and commitment to managing your finances.

6.4. Transforming Mindsets: From a Saver to an Investor

A vital aspect of strategic budgeting involves shifting from being merely a saver to becoming an investor.

Saving is a good financial habit, but it mostly keeps your money idle. Investment, on the other hand, allows your money to generate more money over time. It could be stocks, bonds, mutual funds, real estate, or even building your own business.

By incorporating investments into your budget, you're not just allocating resources for current expenses, but you're also directing money toward income-generation ventures that can bring you closer to financial freedom.

Strategic budgeting is a journey and not a quick fix. It calls for patient effort, regular refinement, and, certainly, a commitment to your financial goals. But if implemented well, it can bring about a significant transformation in your financial well-being.

Lastly, remember that monetary tranquility is not only about having tons of money but finding peace and freedom in managing your financial life with confidence. So, whether you're knee-deep in debts or planning your retirement, strategic budgeting can guide you to consistent, fruitful steps toward financial resilience and tranquility.

Chapter 7. Unearthing Money Traps: Take Control of Hidden Financial Stressors

In our quest for financial prosperity, it's easy to fall into money traps that can place unnecessary stress on our mental wellbeing. These traps are sometimes shrouded in the complexity of financial management or disguised as conventional wisdom. Recognizing and overcoming these barriers is a crucial step towards achieving financial tranquility. So let's understand what these hidden financial stressors are and how you can take control of them.

7.1. The Allure of Instant Gratification

A prevalent money trap that can inflict financial stress is the allure of instant gratification. Society and modern media desire us to believe that happiness is just one purchase away. Advertisements are designed to tap into our emotional responses, encouraging impulsive buying behaviors. "Buy now, pay later" seems to be the mantra of the day, but cognitive science suggests it's a hazardous path.

Understanding this trap requires us to better appreciate the psychological mechanism at work. The pleasure principle, rooted in Freudian psychology, surmises that people seek pleasure and avoid pain. Immediate pleasures, such as impulsive shopping, provide a sense of temporary happiness but often lead to long-term financial distress.

So how can you break the cycle? The first step is recognizing your triggers. Identifying the situations, feelings, or environments that provoke impulsive spending can provide insight into your behaviors.

Is it during sales? Is it when you're feeling down? Or perhaps after payday?

Next, consider delayed gratification. Proven through the well-known Stanford marshmallow experiment, those who resist immediate temptation reap long-term benefits. When you next feel the urge to make an unnecessary purchase, challenge yourself to wait. By doing so, you allow room for rational thinking to break through the tempting allure of instant gratification.

7.2. The Debt Cycle

Another significant money trap is the persistent debt cycle. Often, we downplay the long-term consequences of debt due to the immediate benefits it provides. Whether it's credit card bills, student loans, or mortgages, debt can turn into a continual source of stress.

To escape this cycle, you need to get onto solid financial ground. Start by understanding your debts. Organize them by the interest rates and develop a repayment strategy. Paying off high-interest debts first — a method known as the 'avalanche' strategy — could save you significant amounts of money that would otherwise go to interest.

Next, aim to build an emergency fund. Life is unpredictable, and financial surprises arise when we least expect them. A backup reserve can prevent you from falling back into the debt cycle when these situations occur.

Lastly, work on fostering a healthy relationship with credit. It's not about completely eliminating debt but learning how to use it strategically. Understand your credit score, know how it's calculated, and take measures to improve and maintain it.

7.3. Lifestyle Inflation

As we progress in our careers and incomes rise, lifestyle inflation often comes into play. It involves increasing our spending as our earnings grow, leading to a perpetual cycle where saving feels impossible despite higher wages. The critical thing to remember is that wealth is not about the money earned but about the money saved.

To combat lifestyle inflation, start tracking your expenses and income. Proper budgeting can help you understand the influx of your money, thereby giving you control over it. Incremental upgrades to your lifestyle may not seem significant individually, but they can add up.

Moreover, as your income increases, consider increasing your savings too. As a rule of thumb, part of every financial windfall, including pay raises and bonuses, should go towards savings and investments.

7.4. The Fear of Investing

Investing can be daunting. The markets can indeed be volatile, and the fear of losing money often keeps people from entering this world of potential wealth creation. However, investing, if done wisely and with patience, can be an incredibly potent tool for financial wellness.

Begin by educating yourself. Familiarize yourself with investment concepts, types of investments, market trends, and risks associated. Numerous resources can help you grasp these complexities, empowering you to make more informed decisions.

In addition, diversifying your investments can ensure that market fluctuations do not wipe away your savings entirely. As the saying goes, 'do not put all your eggs in one basket'. Spread your investments across different vehicle types to minimize risk.

Lastly, remember the principle of compound interest. It can seem insignificant in short-term periods but incredibly powerful over the long term. Investment isn't a quick fix but rather a long-term strategy for financial security.

Overcoming these money traps is key to your journey towards financial tranquility. By gaining awareness of these hidden stressors and taking preventative steps, you can navigate these pitfalls and foster a financially healthier mindset. Remember, the goal is not merely wealth creation, but realizing a future of financial security with an energized spirit. With careful planning, discipline, and knowledge, you'll be well on your way to financial resilience and empowerment.

Chapter 8. Investing In You: The Power of Personal Finance Education

Educating oneself in personal finance is akin to a getting a lifetime ticket to the train of wealth creation and financial stability. The advantages are multifold, and its essence can be felt in various facets of life, including debt management, investment, budgeting, and retirement planning. The true power of personal finance education extends beyond the sheets of balance, it touches upon the psychological aspects, instilling discipline, stress management, and decision-making efficacy.

8.1. The Case for Financial Education

Familiarity with personal finance equates to not merely weathering through financial bumps but foreseeing, planning for, and efficiently navigating through these fiscal challenges. Anecdotal evidence and research alike illuminate how individuals with a robust understanding of personal finance are at an advantage. They exhibit skilled budgeting, are less likely to be entrapped in cycles of debt, and more prone to thoughtful investing. In a society laden with financial choices, the beacon light of personal financial education enlightens the path of sound monetary decision-making.

Financial education molds the mindset that wealth is not an overnight accomplishment, but a gradual, methodical result of smart choices and informed decisions. It plays a pivotal role in distinguishing good debt from bad, enabling understanding, and the managament of one's credit score.

8.2. Understanding Money

Money is not just a medium of exchange but a dynamic tool that can be leveraged to achieve desired financial goals. Standing on three foundational pillars - Earning, spending, and saving/investing, understanding money involves comprehending this trinity in an integrated manner.

Consider earning: a salaried job will net you a stable income, whereas a business or freelancing venture may offer variable returns. Dividend-paying stocks or bonds bring in passive income. Comprehending the nature and the timing of these income streams adequately prepares one for budgeting and further investment planning.

Effective spending can be achieved by devising a reasonable budget. An insightful financial education strives to equip individuals with knowledge on the nature of expenses- fixed, discretionary, and unexpected. The art of cutting down on irrelevant expenses and prioritizing desires paves the way for a healthier spending program.

The power of compounding lies at the heart of investing. Personal finance literacy underscores the idea of making your money work for you. Understanding different investment mediums, their risks, and returns form a crucial aspect of personal finance education.

8.3. Debt Management

Debt can be a double-edged sword. Managed well, it can provide that much-needed push in matters of investment opportunities or critical emergencies. Mishandled debt often leads to financial stress and, in extreme cases, bankruptcy. The role of personal finance education in this context is distinguished.

It begins with comprehending various debt options like car loans, home loans, credit card debts, and student loans, each carrying different interest percentages and term conditions. It aids in understanding the cost of borrowing and helps individuals create bulletproof plans for timely repayment.

8.4. Investing Wisely

Investment is the footbridge that connects present income with future financial goals. However, it is filled with choices. Stocks, bonds, mutual funds, real estate, and gold are likely to feature in your investment horizon. Personal finance education demystifies these options and aids in choosing the suitable one aligning with one's risk appetite, return expectation, and time horizon. It aids in devising a diverse investment portfolio, thereby mitigating risk and enhancing potential returns.

8.5. Retirement Planning

Most individuals dream of comfortable, stress-free sunset years. However, dreams don't transpire without strategic actions. Personal finance education ramps up retirement readiness. It aids in understanding the power of early and disciplined investing and enlightens on the available options like pension schemes, retirement accounts (IRA, 401k), and annuities, to name a few.

8.6. Conclusion

Feeling empowered about managing money is not merely about securing a financially stable future. It's about having the freedom to make conscious monetary decisions aligned with life goals. Educating oneself in personal finance is like driving your vehicle; you take control, navigate turns, and reach the destination. Personal finance education is that GPS in your monetary vehicle, ensuring the course in this journey is not tiresomely navigated, but wisely taken. It truly is an investment in one's growth, empowerment, and long-term financial well-being. After all, financial literacy is not an end in itself, but a means to various ends like financial stability, wealth creation, stress-free retirement, and of course, the resultant peace of mind.

Chapter 9. Financial Resilience: Bouncing Back from Financial Setbacks

Financial resilience is about more than just surviving financial setbacks; it's about thriving in the face of them. While it's impossible to predict and completely prevent each and every financial bump in the road, we can arm ourselves with tools that allow us to bounce back and stay on track with our financial goals. This chapter provides strategies to cultivate financial resilience.

9.1. Building a Financial Safety Net

The first step towards achieving financial resilience is establishing a financial safety net. This typically takes the form of an emergency savings fund. Advisors commonly recommend keeping three to six months' worth of living expenses stashed away in an easily accessible account. This buffer ensures that you can remain financially steady even when faced with unexpected expenses.

Assembling such a fund might seem daunting, but it's manageable when broken down into smaller steps. Here are some suggestions:

- Identify the monthly expenses that are essential for your survival, such as food, housing, utilities, etc.

- Determine the amount that needs to be saved to cover these expenses for a three to six-month period.

- Create a savings plan, reserving a specific portion of your income each month towards building your fund.

- Automate these savings if possible. This ensures regular contributions and eliminates the temptation to skip a deposit.

9.2. Investing in Insurance

Aside from an emergency fund, another significant component of the financial safety net is insurance. Different types of insurance protect against various kinds of financial risks – health insurance for medical emergencies, homeowners insurance for property damages, and life insurance for maintaining the financial standards of dependent family members in case of an unfortunate event.

Understanding your personal risk factors and obtaining appropriate coverage is crucial in minimizing financial vulnerabilities. Carry out an examination of different insurance products available in the market. Understand the coverage, premiums, deductibles, and terms and conditions before deciding on one.

9.3. Diversifying Your Portfolio

Much like the well-known saying, "don't put all your eggs in one basket", diversifying your portfolio can significantly reduce the risk associated with investing. Portfolio diversification refers to spreading out your investments across various asset classes such as stocks, bonds, real estate, commodities, etc.

In the event of a downturn in one sector, losses are balanced against gains in another, creating a safety net for your investments. Consult with a financial advisor or execute your own research to understand which investment vehicles work best for your specific circumstances.

9.4. Cultivating a Growth Mindset

One of the most underestimated aspects of financial resilience is the mindset. Cultivating a growth mindset, coined by psychologist Carol Dweck, is critical. This refers to the belief that one's abilities and intelligence can be developed through dedication and hard work.

When it comes to personal finances, a growth mindset enables us to learn from financial setbacks rather than being daunted by them. Therefore, using a setback as a stepping stone for improvement primes you for future challenges and helps develop resilience.

9.5. Debt Management Strategy

Debt can be an enormous source of financial stress, and it can hinder your progress towards financial resilience. It's critical to develop a strategy for effectively managing and eventually eliminating your debt.

Here's a basic idea of how to formulate a debt management strategy:

- Make a list of all your debts, including information such as the creditor, total amount of the debt, monthly payment, and due date.

- Prioritize your debts. This could be done using the 'avalanche method' – paying off the more expensive debts first, or the 'snowball method' – paying off smaller debts first to build momentum.

- Commit to making the minimum payments on every debt.

- Determine any additional money you can put towards debts after covering your essential living expenses. Put this towards the top priority debt while making minimum payments on the rest.

- Once the top priority debt is paid off, move to the next priority, and follow the same strategy.

The most important aspect of debt management is consistency, discipline, and patience. Just like every worthwhile journey, financial resilience takes time and persistence.

9.6. Regular Financial Review

A pivotal part of achieving financial resilience involves regularly reviewing your financial situation. This involves keeping track of your earnings, spending, savings, investments, and debt. By regularly examining your finances, you can understand your spending habits, identify areas for improvement, and make timely decisions to ensure you remain on track towards building financial resilience.

In conclusion, building financial resilience is not a quick fix process – it's a long-term commitment. But by employing the strategies mentioned in this chapter, you can turn financial setbacks into opportunities for growth and advancement, strengthening your personal economy and paving the way for a financially tranquil future. The more prepared you are, the less daunting any setback seems, and the quicker you recover. Keep this in mind as you cultivate your resilience and continue on your journey towards financial well-being.

Chapter 10. Cultivating Prosperity: Mindful Habits for Sustainable Wealth

Building rewarding habits that promote financial prosperity is an undertaking that combines resourcefulness, determination, and a discerning eye. Insightful money management involves deliberate decisions around saving, investing, and spending. When paired with mindfulness, these economic activities morph into conscious actions triggering prosperity and a sustainable wealth model. Let's delve into the secrets of cultivating financial abundance through mindful habits.

10.1. A Mindful Approach to Saving

Mindfulness, when applied to saving, brings awareness to your thoughts and decisions revolving around money. To be mindful means to act with consideration, focusing on each individual action, aware of its impact on the bigger picture.

Understanding the difference between your needs and wants is the first step towards conscious saving. Needs are things you must have for survival, like food and shelter, while wants are things you desire or crave. Just by recognizing these aspects, you can redistribute your funds more efficiently.

Consider automating your savings. Make a choice at the onset about how much of your income you want to save each month, and immediately transfer this portion when you receive your paycheck. It makes savings a priority, not an afterthought.

10.2. Diversifying and Mindful Investing

When it comes to investment, diversity is your ally. Distributing your funds across various investment options can help minimize risk. You should not put all your financial eggs into one basket.

> Start small, perhaps in low-risk investments like certificates of deposit, money market accounts, or government bonds. Little by little, expand your portfolio into assets like stocks and mutual funds. It's about preserving the capital while targeting reasonable returns.

Remember to research and fully understand the investment vehicle you're considering. Knowledge is power; investing without it can lead to avoidable losses. Moreover, be alert to market changes and stay updated about economic news, as these can influence the performance of your investments.

10.3. Conscious Spending: Putting Your Money Where Your Values Lie

Conscious spending isn't about strict budgeting; it is about making deliberate decisions aligned with your values and financial goals. It involves questioning each expenditure: Do I need this? Why am I buying it? Is there an alternative that aligns better with my goals?

Prioritize spending on experiences over material possessions. Studies indicate that people derive more happiness from experiences than from things. Plus, by limiting unnecessary purchases, you may find you have more money to invest or save.

Commit yourself to becoming a savvy consumer. Implement strategies like comparing prices before purchasing, waiting for sales, and not being swayed by discounts on items you don't need.

10.4. Building Resilience through Financial Education

Being financially literate empowers you to lead a financially sound life. Grasping concepts such as interest rates, investment risk, and the time value of money enable you to make informed decisions.

Don't shy away from asking for help if needed. Connect with financial advisors, read relevant books, take courses, or attend seminars. Expanding your knowledge base is investing in yourself.

Always be aware of any changes in financial trends, legislation, and markets. Resilience is also about being adaptable.

10.5. Mindful Habits for Retirement Planning

Start planning for retirement as early as possible. A steadfast dedication to this long-term goal sets the stage for a comfortable post-career lifestyle.

One common method is harnessing the power of compound interest, a phenomenon where your interest earns more interest. When started early, even a small investment can grow wildly in the long run.

Don't overlook protection. Investing in relevant insurance policies safeguards your hard-earned assets. Don't allow a medical or personal crisis to erode your accumulated wealth.

In conclusion putting mindfulness at the heart of your financial decisions promotes nurturing habits, encouraging saving, wise investing, conscious spending, continuous learning, and meticulous planning. Embracing these principles fosters sustainable wealth and prosperity, navigating you towards a financially secure future marked by tranquility and resilience. Dive into the journey of exploration, commitment, and growth. The prosperity you seek is not a distant dream, but a well-planned destination.

Chapter 11. Strengthening Financial Wellness: Bridging the Gap to Your Future Security

Our financial health is intrinsically linked to our mental well-being. It's a critical aspect of overall wellness yet so often found neglected due to complexities, discomfort, or lack of insight. This chapter serves as your detailed guide to enhancing your financial security through building and maintaining a financially healthy mindset and implementing proven, effective financial strategies. It explores steps for achieving financial resilience and empowerment, with a route to tranquility in your financial journey.

11.1. Understanding the Origin of Financial Stress

Stress about finances doesn't materialize overnight. It is often a by-product of a prolonged pattern of unaddressed financial issues, fear, and an unclear path to resolution. To bridge the gap to future security, it's crucial first to identify what's causing your financial stress.

- Job instability or low income

- High levels of debt

- Unplanned emergencies

- Insufficient savings

- Retirement insecurities

Once identified, it's easier to develop a targeted strategy to mitigate these stressors and prevent them from negatively impacting your financial wellness in the future.

11.2. Building a Resilient Financial Strategy

Financial resilience isn't just about surviving; it's about thriving in the face of adversity. It requires contingency planning, smart investing, and the ability to adapt financially to life's unexpected disruptions.

- **Budgeting**: A well-structured budget helps you understand where your money is going and provides a roadmap for financial decisions. Delineate income, expenses, and saving goals in an accessible format to visualize your financial health accurately.

- **Emergency Fund**: This serves as your financial safety net in times of crisis. Endeavor to save at least three to six months' worth of living expenses.

- **Debt Reduction Plan**: Depending on the scale of your debt, different approaches like debt avalanche (highest interest first) or debt snowball (smallest amount first) could be implemented.

- **Investing for Growth**: Investing can help you build wealth. Learning the basics about stocks, bonds, mutual funds, real estate, and following a diversified investment strategy can go a long way.

- **Insurances**: Protect yourself financially with the right insurances. Health, life, car, home insurances can shield you from unexpected and significant expenses.

- **Retirement Planning**: Start retirement planning as early as possible, considering factors like living expenses, desired lifestyle, and healthcare costs.

11.3. Recognizing and Changing Negative Financial Behaviors

Self-awareness is key to changing financial behaviors that are detrimental to your financial health. Track your spending habits, evaluate needs versus wants, and curtail impulse purchases by implementing strategies like the 24-hour rule (waiting 24 hours before making a non-essential purchase). Avoid emotional spending, and hit the pause button on your credit card usage if it tends to lead to overspending.

11.4. Financial Literacy: Your Key to Empowerment

Understanding financial concepts elevates your confidence in making informed decisions about your money. It's about learning and continuing to educate yourself on different financial topics. Resources like blogs, podcasts, books, online courses can contribute significantly to expanding your knowledge.

11.5. Emotional Wellness in Finance

Financial decisions aren't free from emotional influence. Fear, anxiety, guilt are just a few emotions that might cloud judgment. Incorporating mindful practices like meditation and breathing exercises can help manage these emotions.

Seeing financial matters as an integral part of our overall wellness and not a separate entity helps us to create a harmonious financial life. It's about achieving financial serenity while maintaining emotional balance.

Ultimately, the journey to a confident and financially savvy life is a long one, filled with learning, adjustments, and patience. Embrace the process, honoring every step forward and learning from any setbacks. Adopt a growth mindset, understanding that your financial wellness is a constant journey, not a destination. With these practices and perspectives in mind, you're well on the way to bridging the gap to your future security.